T0367252

Retirement:

A New Adventure

|||||||||||||||||||||||||||||||||||||||||||||||||||||||||||||||||||||||||||||||||||||||||||||||||||||||||

Retirement:
A New Adventure

|||||||||||||||||||||||||||||||||||||||||||||||||||||||||||||||||||||||||||||||||

CHRISTOPHER BORMAN

iUniverse, Inc.
New York Bloomington

Retirement
A New Adventure

iUniverse books may be ordered through booksellers or by contacting:

iUniverse
1663 Liberty Drive
Bloomington, IN 47403
www.iuniverse.com
1-800-Authors (1-800-288-4677)

ISBN: 978-1-4401-6802-4 (sc)
ISBN: 978-1-4401-6804-8 (dj)
ISBN: 978-1-4401-6803-1 (ebk)

Library of Congress Control Number: 2009936190

Printed in the United States of America

iUniverse rev. date: 09/22/2009

Contents

Acknowledgments

There are many individuals who contributed to the writing of this book. I want to thank the people who completed the retirement questionnaires. Their time and insights are appreciated. Also, the individuals who sat for the case studies devoted considerable time to this project, and the doctoral students who assisted me in the case studies deserve thanks.

My life has been blessed by having a wonderful family, especially my wife, Ruth. She has devoted considerable time and effort to this book—typing, editing, and revising. Also, our daughter, Claire, assisted in preparing the manuscript.

Introduction

As a university professor in the field of counseling psychology, I have been thinking about and planning to write a book on retirement for several years. With a doctorate in counseling, I taught at Texas A&M University (College Station) for twenty-one years and then at The University of Texas–San Antonio for thirteen years. I am currently Professor Emeritus at UT San Antonio.

Before receiving my doctorate and my university teaching experience, I was a counselor at Technical-Vocational High School in Hammond, Indiana for six years. My interest in career counseling evolved in this position as I found that many students had no idea what they wanted to do as a career. Many of them probably ended up going to work in the local steel mills or oil refineries like their parents. My early involvement with young people making career decisions spurred my interest within the field of counseling to the concentrations of career counseling and career development. I have published numerous articles in areas relating to career counseling. Also, I have become very interested in descriptive research and case studies that describe the career experiences of individuals.

It has been a long and interesting journey from working with high school students to retirees. In this book I attempt to describe actual experiences of people as they planned for retirement and then what they experienced when they retired.

Just as students need a plan for starting a career, I think that everyone needs a plan for retirement. After a lifetime of work, it is fitting that your later years will be fulfilling and enjoyable. Even if you are already retired, you can still develop a plan. As you read the following chapters, you will find information on how others went from careers to retirement to positive adventures. The first chapter deals with the longevity attitude. Research shows that longevity is related more to lifestyle and attitude than heredity. Suggestions are given for developing a healthy attitude.

A major portion of the book relates my experiences as I planned for retirement and the experiences of eighteen retirees who completed a questionnaire about their retirement experiences. Also, I have included in-depth case studies of four retirees. Hopefully, as you read through the case studies, you will find a similarity to your own career and life situation. You will see how others have made decisions and plans that may be beneficial to you in making retirement plans. I hope that you find this book interesting and useful as you plan and/or experience retirement.

Chapter 1
The Longevity Attitude

IIIIIIIIIIIIIIIIIIIIIIIIIIIIIIIIIIIIIIIIIIIIIIIIIIIIIIIIIIIIIIIIIIIIIIIIIIIIIIIIIIIIIIIIIIIIIIIIIIIIIIIIIIIIIIIIIIIIIIIIIIIIIIIIIIIIIIIIIIIIIIIIIIII

In 1998, David Mahoney, a businessman and advocate of
brain research, and Richard Restak, M.D., a neurologist and
psychiatrist, published a book entitled *The Longevity Strategy:
How to Live to 100 Using the Brain-Body Connection*. They
made the point that heredity is responsible for only about
one-quarter of the variation in human life spans. The rest of
the variation is due to living healthy and productive lives. In
collecting information for their book, Mahoney and Restak
talked to Stanley Jacobson, a seventy-five-year-old clinical
psychologist specializing in working with elderly clients.
Jacobson identified traits that assist people in aging gracefully,
such as basic optimism, adaptability, readiness to take
responsibility, resilience, involvement in meaningful projects
and relationships, and healthy self-esteem.

In their book, Mahoney and Restak (1998) offered many suggestions for living longer, such as optimism. They indicated that optimists live better and longer lives. Also, it is healthy to have a sense of humor. Self-help books, counseling literature, and other sources have indicated for years the benefits of a sense of humor. The authors also identified three factors that put individuals at risk for life-threatening ailments: (1) hostility, (2) depression, and (3) social isolation.

A *Parade Magazine* article by Lou Ann Walker in 2001 focused on a Harvard study directed by Dr. George E. Vaillant that studied 824 men and women between sixty and eighty years of age. This study is one of the longest and most comprehensive studies of human development ever undertaken. The study found four attributes that contribute to successful aging:

1. Orientation toward the future
2. Gratitude, forgiveness, and optimism
3. Empathy for the feelings of others
4. The ability to reach out

A major finding was that good genes and money do not account for better aging. The way individuals live their lives determines how well they age.

Dr. Vaillant identified seven factors that at age fifty predict what life's outcome will be at age eighty:

1. Not smoking
2. The ability to take life's ups and downs in stride
3. Absence of alcohol abuse
4. Healthy weight
5. A solid marriage
6. Physical activity
7. Years of education—the more, the better

He said that people who had four or more of these seven factors at age fifty were one-third less likely to be dead at age eighty.

There are many examples of individuals who have adjusted well to retirement or decided not to retire and are doing well in their later years. Jack Frankel had a long and successful career as a scientist, researcher, founder of the Lawrence Livermore National Laboratory, and university president (*Bryan-College Station Eagle* 1985). At age sixty-one, he quit his job as a university president to become an actor because he thought that it would be fun. In a newspaper article, he described his enthusiasm over a bit part in a movie. At age one hundred, Grace Berry was still working for a weekly newspaper in

Thorndale, Texas, and enjoying herself not because she had to work but because it was fun.

There are also many examples of individuals who did not have a plan for retirement and are leading lives that will probably not lead to longevity. In a 2005 article in the *Houston Chronicle*, Larry McShane of the Associated Press described the exploits of Dan Freeman, retired, who set out to visit a thousand bars in a single year. Freeman, a retired computer consultant, launched a blog about his experiences. He was not out to get drunk and usually had only one drink at each bar. At the time of the newspaper article, he had visited five hundred bars and felt that he was on track to visit one thousand bars in a year.

More older workers are deciding it is not time to clock out just yet (Christoffersen 2007). John Christoffersen, a newspaper columnist, talked about Pete Perillo, ninety-two, who is still working as a guard at the city courthouse in Stamford, Connecticut. Christoffersen also told of Grace Wiles, ninety-seven, who works twenty-five hours a week at a shoe repair store in Maryland, and Sally Gordon, ninety-eight, who is the legislature's assistant sergeant-at-arms in Nebraska. Waldo McBurney at one hundred four, who is a beekeeper from Kansas, was declared America's oldest worker.

About 6.4 percent of adults in the United States age seventy-five or older, or slightly more than one million, were working in 2006 (Christoffersen 2007). Some older Americans are continuing to work because they have to work as a result of reduced or limited pensions, but many are continuing to work because they want to remain active and be with people. Retirees seek work that is meaningful and stimulating, and that offers them opportunities to make differences in others' lives (Freedman 2001). Winston Churchill's philosophy was expressed by the statement, "Never, never, never retire" (Maloney and Restak 1998, 158).

Chapter 2
Deciding to Retire:
My Experience

I had been thinking about retirement from my university position for a while, and as I got ready for the new fall semester, I decided to make an appointment with my financial advisor to see if I had enough funds to retire. This meeting included my wife, who was already drawing teacher's retirement and Social Security. I was drawing Social Security benefits since I was sixty-nine years old at the time. We thought that we had sufficient value in our mutual fund accounts to live comfortably, and our meeting with the financial advisor was very reassuring. She told us that our financial situation was very favorable for a comfortable retirement.

Letting People Know

With the financial situation looking favorable, I decided that the coming school year would be my last. Having worked in higher education for a long time, I knew that the best approach was to let the university administration know about my retirement plans as soon as possible so they would have enough time to recruit a new faculty member for my position. Before the fall semester began, I met with the department chair to tell him about my plans. I did not have to meet with the people in Human Resources until a couple of months before I officially retired.

I did not feel the need to keep my retirement a secret, so I did not hesitate to discuss it with colleagues and students. My area of specialty in the counseling field has been career development, and I was teaching two sections of a graduate course on career counseling and development. During the part of the course on adults in career transition, I mentioned my impending retirement, but I did not want to dwell on it. Both colleagues and students seemed supportive of my plans and frequently wanted to know what I was going to do after retirement.

Expectations

My hope was to have my final year of teaching as normal and routine as possible. My teaching schedule involved teaching two sections of a graduate level course on career development and career counseling. I also served on several university committees, including several tenure and promotion committees and a search committee. An important part of a faculty member's responsibilities is advising students, and I was advisor for a large number (60–70) of master's degree students majoring in counseling.

Another important responsibility at a university is research and publishing articles on the research. I continued my research activities by having an article published in a national journal. It is also important to remain active in professional organizations, and I made a research presentation at a state convention in the fall. Besides having a good crowd and response to my presentation, attendance at the convention gave me an opportunity to visit with old friends and colleagues. My teaching, research, and advising activities were very similar to what I had been doing for many years.

Feelings

When the fall semester began, I felt a great relief because it would be the last year that I would commute to my job. We had sold our house and bought a house in another city about two hundred miles away. This move was made when my wife retired as an elementary school teacher. Our new house was close to our daughters and grandchildren, but it meant that I commuted each week to my job at the university. I became adjusted to the travel, but when the last year began, it was good to know that the travel would soon end.

In terms of realizing that I would be ending my role as a university professor, I did not have any special feelings when the fall semester began. When the spring semester started in January, I felt satisfied with my decision to retire. One change that I noticed in my feelings about my job was some frustration at faculty meetings that not much was being constructively accomplished.

My plans for retirement included volunteer work or a part-time job or business. One opportunity was volunteer work and involvement at our church. The year prior to my retirement, I participated in a thirty-six-week Bible study and group experience. Then I was supposed to teach and lead a similar group the next year; however, not enough people signed up to participate. This meant that I did not have a group to lead, and I was very disappointed.

Unexpected Events

Although my last year at the university was rather routine and what I had expected, there were some happenings that I had not expected. The university had a main campus and a newer downtown campus. With most of the department faculty at the downtown campus and my office on the main campus, it was suggested by the department chair that I might move to be with the rest of the faculty. It was not required that I move my office, but I decided to move. This move required some work and inconvenience, but it gave me an opportunity to discard many books and papers in anticipation of retirement. The new office was very comfortable and in a new building.

As the fall semester began, I received a call from the dean at a university close to our new home. He needed someone to teach a couple of graduate counseling courses and wanted to know if I was available. I told him that I was still employed full-time but would be retiring. He told me that teaching for him after I retired would be an option. This telephone conversation was very encouraging for me because my retirement plans involved remaining active in my profession at a reduced rate.

I was asked by our dean to serve as university marshal for the December commencement. This is a special honor to lead the academic procession into the field house for the commencement ceremony. It was a very rewarding experience for me.

Everything was going as expected in terms of my teaching schedule when the spring semester began in mid-January. During the first week of the semester, I met my classes, and we discussed the scope of the courses, reading assignments, and course requirements. The students in each course seemed receptive, and I said that I would see them the next week. Little did I know that on the weekend I would have a bicycle accident that would cause me to miss five weeks of classes. I broke my right ankle and required surgery and the placement of screws and a piece of metal in the ankle. This was a painful experience and required a number of lifestyle changes, including the fact that I could not drive my car. Fortunately, the department chair was able to hire an adjunct faculty member to take my place.

After five weeks of not meeting my classes, I decided that I needed to return to class because it would not be fair to the students if I stayed out much longer. Since I could not drive, my wife drove me to the university and stayed overnight with me while I taught my classes. First, I used a wheelchair and then a walker. The semester only had about four weeks remaining when I had recovered enough to drive by myself. The adjunct faculty member had done an excellent job of teaching my classes, and I was able to resume teaching without any difficulty. The students were very supportive, and I enjoyed working with both classes. In fact, on the last day of classes, they had a surprise party including cake to mark my retirement.

During the time that my ankle was in a cast, I celebrated my seventieth birthday, and my family had a nice party for me. At the time, I was feeling my age because of limited mobility with the ankle injury. At the end of the semester, the department had a retirement luncheon for me, which was very much appreciated.

Life Since Retirement

It is four years since I retired, and I have enjoyed my less hectic schedule. However, I took a part-time job teaching graduate courses at the university whose dean had called just before I retired. This teaching opportunity gave me the chance to stay active in my field.

The first fall, my wife and I took a trip to Catalina Island and then to Santa Barbara. We flew to California and rented a car. The following summer, we took a trip to Alaska that included a seven-day cruise. Again, we flew there and back. The next summer, my wife and I flew to Rome and took an eleven-day cruise of the western Mediterranean and a number of land tours in Monaco, France, Italy, Spain, and Tunisia. Neither one of us had ever taken such a trip in terms of distance and number of countries visited, and we had a wonderful time except for some luggage being lost.

This past spring and summer, we have not done as much traveling, except for a couple of trips to California to visit our first grandson, who was one year old in October. We also just returned from an airplane trip to Indiana for a family wedding. During the Indiana trip, we spent a day in Bloomington visiting the Indiana University campus that we had both attended. It was nice to visit special sites on the campus and reminisce.

My goal is to stay active and healthy as long as I can. About three years ago, I joined a health club, and I exercise with weight machines three to four days a week for about two hours each session. The days that I am not at the gym, I ride my bicycle in the neighborhood for about fifty minutes. During the past three years, I have tried to adopt the "Longevity Attitude" by eating a healthy diet, exercising, and handling stress effectively. I feel much better since I retired, and I have lost over forty pounds.

I am not sure how long I will continue teaching two graduate courses a semester for the local university. This fall I am beginning my fourth year teaching these courses. I enjoy the teaching and interacting with the graduate students. However, I am thinking that I might want to do some volunteer work associated with our church. For two of the three years that I have been retired, I have taken long-term Bible courses (36 week courses). Consequently, spirituality and serving God are important considerations for me. Also, my wife and I have just booked a river cruise on the Danube, which starts in Hungary and ends in Germany. We have added three days at the end to visit Prague.

Chapter 3
Survey of Retirees

IIIIIIIIIIIIIIIIIIIIIIIIIIIIIIIIIIIIIIIIIIIIIIIIIIIIIIIIIIIIIIIIIIIIIIIIIIIIIIIIIIIIIIIIIIIIIIIIIIIIIIIIIIIIIIIIIIIIIIIIIIIIIIIIIIIIIIII

After experiencing retirement myself, I decided to collect information from other retirees to see what their experiences had been. My method for collecting this information was to develop a four-item questionnaire that I would ask retirees to complete. The items were open-ended and meant to have the respondents describe their experiences. The study was of a descriptive nature and not meant to generate numbers and conclusions based on statistical analysis. Also, the items required some time to complete, so it took a while to get enough individuals to complete the questionnaire (ultimately eighteen retirees responded to the questionnaire). Since I was a former educator myself, more educators completed the questionnaire than individuals from other occupational categories.

The cover page of the questionnaire had a brief description of the study and indicated that information on respondents would be kept confidential. Also, my name, address, phone number, and e-mail address were listed if anyone had questions or concerns about the study. Each of the four items was printed on a separate page (front and back), and a blank page was at the end of the document if they needed extra space. The respondents were encouraged to add other pages if needed. The four items were the following:

1. Describe briefly your work experience and especially your work prior to retirement.
2. Describe the process that you went through in deciding to retire.
3. What have you been doing since retirement in regards to expectations, life changes, activities, and health matters?
4. Would you like to discuss any spiritual considerations in your lifestyle and expectations?

Two retired university professors completed the questionnaire. One had been a professor in the teacher education program at a major university. The other person had taught masters and doctoral level courses in a counseling program at the same university. He also had a small private practice as a counseling psychologist, but he was retired from both positions.

Among the six public school respondents, one had been a classroom teacher, an assistant principal for two years, a reading specialist for five years, and a program coordinator for eight years. Another person had worked in public schools with special needs students, and one respondent had been a middle school teacher for over thirty years. Another teacher taught in an elementary school, including twenty-three years in the sixth grade. The other two educators ended their careers as principals. One was a business education teacher and spent the last ten years as a principal. The other person started out as a high school social studies teacher, spent four years as an elementary school principal, and then eighteen years as a middle school principal.

One retiree stated that he had been a stocker at a liquor store and had spent twenty-six years as a forklift operator in a plant. One woman started her career as a housewife and then spent thirty-four years as a nurse in various health care areas, retiring as a school nurse. Another nurse did medical interpreting before she retired. She did this job for twenty-two years, and it required considerable travel. A retired physician said that he had specialized in pediatrics. One respondent said that he was a driver for food companies and then for Exxon while serving part-time as a church pastor. One woman had various jobs in a cotton mill, maid services, a restaurant, and Federal Express. A systems engineering manager of an air traffic control system also completed the questionnaire. A mother with five sons and three daughters worked in the food service department of a school and then in the classroom as a para educator after her children were in school. One man worked in an industrial plant as a laborer and forklift operator and then completed his career as a custodian. Another retiree worked for Exxon Mobil for forty-three years as a plant operator supervising workers. Finally, a worker for 3M Company was in sales and marketing for thirty-one years selling data recording equipment to oil companies.

Chapter 4
Reasons for Retiring

||||||||||||||||||||||||||||||||||||||||||||||||||||||||||||||||||||||||||||||||||||||||||||||||||||||||||||||||||||||||||||||||||||||||||||||||||

The two retirees who were from the same university had different reasons for retiring. One professor thought about retiring, but the dean asked him to write a new curriculum for the elementary teacher preparation program. He delayed his retirement and wrote the curriculum; however, when the new curriculum was finished and making its way through the various university committees for approval, the dean did not lend support to the approval process. This occurrence upset the professor, and he retired immediately. The other university professor taught graduate level counseling courses and also had a small private counseling practice in the community. He had been thinking about retirement, and his wife who also had a Ph.D. was offered a job in another city. They decided that he would retire from his university position but start a small private practice in the new location. He had his private practice for several years until his wife was offered a position close to where they had lived previously, so they moved again and he retired permanently with no private practice.

A pastor and his wife each completed the questionnaire. Although he had worked full-time as a pastor, he also worked another job to support his family. Finally, he grew weary of working two jobs, so he quit his other job to devote his energy solely to being a pastor. His wife quit her job before she was 50 so she could spend more time with her son and daughter.

Robert (not his real name) was a retired physician who was a pediatrician and enjoyed his work. However, he decided to retire because of problems with managed care and the cost of malpractice insurance. Robert's children had completed college, and he had built a nest egg, so he did not have to worry about finances.

Two businessmen who completed the questionnaire were retired because their companies offered excellent retirement packages. John (all names have been changed) had worked for IBM, and he said that the company offered a retirement incentive that was too good to ignore. James had worked for 3M Company, and when he met the company retirement age of fifty-nine and one-half years, he retired. James was assured of an adequate pension and good medical insurance for him and his wife.

One respondent said that he retired because all bills were paid including his house and his health was failing. A woman retired because her husband had retired and wanted her to spend quality time with him. Also, she wanted to stay home and take care of her youngest grandson. Jack had mixed emotions about retiring and found the process difficult. He thought about his health and finances, and work in the factory was getting more difficult, so Jack finally decided to retire. Donald, before retiring, prayed and asked God for direction. He also talked to his wife, who encouraged him to retire because of the many years that he had worked.

Several of the respondents who were teachers retired because of Social Security benefits. One teacher retired because it was the last year that she could retire and be eligible for her husband's Social Security. Another teacher said that the Social Security benefits helped him decide to retire. Mary said that her husband had already retired and she was working with older students who had learning difficulties. The work was challenging and difficult, so she decided that it was time to retire. After evaluating Social Security benefits and Teacher Retirement benefits, Diane decided that she could live on her income after retirement. Also, the school district offered a good early retirement package. Being divorced and her children being independent, Diane had the freedom to make her own choices. One factor that encouraged Diane to retire was that she frequently did not agree with the latest teaching trends.

A couple who were principals each answered the questionnaire. Rhonda was a teacher and then a principal, and she said that she prayed throughout her career. Rhonda retired when the campus where she worked was being closed. She said that she retired happy, positive, and successful. Her husband, Stanley, retired the same year and gave two reasons for retiring: (1) he met the teacher retirement formula and was not gaining much financially by continuing to work; (2) he had burned out—eighteen years as a middle school principal was enough.

Joan began thinking about retirement when she realized that her retirement benefits would change very little if she continued to teach. Also, she was not enjoying teaching as much as she had in the past because of having to prepare students for the state testing program. However, Joan's main reason for considering retirement was that she had begun dating a retired businessman who enjoyed doing many recreational activities, and she wanted to spend more time with him. Therefore, Joan did retire.

Chapter 5
Retirement Experiences

The respondents' answers to what they have been doing since retirement were very open and honest. Some have been very busy while others have slowed their pace. For instance, one retired educator has been very active as a tutor, and she opened a day-care center at her church. Also, she is the music director at her church. She and her husband were building a house close to the water that would eventually be a retirement home. Her comment was that health matters have not been a concern.

A retired university professor said that he and his wife had traveled to such places as Russia, Italy, and a number of places in the United States. Their church work included a year-long mission trip. Also, they devoted time to their children and families. His wife never finished her B.S. degree, so he was supporting her in this endeavor. During his spare time, he was writing and reading fiction and history books. At age seventy-four, this retiree said that he was starting to feel the pains of aging and was in close contact with doctors. He thought about death often—sometimes with fear, other times as a natural event.

One person said that he has enjoyed life during retirement and does not long for past employments. To him retirement has been much more pleasant than anticipated. Of most importance has been the close bond between him and his wife. Since his wife was still employed after he retired, he took on many household duties and enjoys them. His contentment is clouded a bit by health concerns. He said, "They serve as a reminder that this too shall pass."

Because one of the retired teachers lost her Social Security benefits (due to the new Windfall Policy which means that you cannot receive Social Security benefits and teacher retirement benefits at the same time), she went back to work full-time. Another teacher said that she is taking care of her grandchildren and does substitute teaching part-time. Her health is still good.

After he retired from IBM, John felt that his accomplishments as an engineer did not satisfy him in terms of helping mankind. This observation was inspired by his Christian beliefs. One month after retirement, John volunteered to do disaster relief work through his church. He spent twelve years doing relief work and felt that the work was very rewarding because of the many people that were helped. John is no longer regional director for disaster services, but he still does consulting work. Osteoarthritis has made a difference in his lifestyle—he is no longer as active physically as he used to be. He has a new hip and had a couple of discs removed, but exercising at a gym has kept him from having further surgeries.

James, a 3M Company retiree, said that since retirement he has maintained a very simple lifestyle—playing golf, working in the yard, exercising, attending church, and enjoying his grandchildren. He and his wife did some traveling, and he feels no pressure, no deadlines, and no quotas or goals. James said that he and his wife keep in touch with old friends.

Being a retired pediatrician qualified Robert to babysit his grandchildren, which he does regularly. He has done some traveling and plays tennis in addition to exercising three times a week. Robert continues to read medical books and visits retired friends. He loves to cook and help his wife shop. However, Robert said that some days he gets bored and depressed and wishes that he never retired. So far, his health has been good.

Since retiring as a principal, Rhonda has been working with student teachers at a local university. Also, she sometimes substitutes as an assistant principal. Rhonda observed that life has not changed much and that she keeps busy and lives a healthy life, going to the gym three times a week. She is in the process of writing a book. When not busy, Rhonda also takes care of her two-year-old grandson. Stanley, Rhonda's husband, who also retired as a principal, has worked as an adjunct professor at a local university. He said that there is never a day that he is not busy and that he exercises at a gym five days a week. Also, he enjoys spending time with his grandson.

A pastor and his wife talked about retirement and their activities. She retired early to spend more time with two younger children and also takes care of her ninety-two-year-old mother. As a pastor's wife, she spends time helping church members in need. She went back to work in retailing to help send her daughter to college and purchase some land where she and her husband plan to retire. Although he is a pastor, her husband never attended school beyond high school. Since retirement he has attended a college of biblical studies to enhance his work as a pastor. He still works part-time in addition to being a minister. Diet and exercise have increased his endurance.

Diane sold her home and has relocated twice to be near family (daughter, husband, and two grandchildren). Being divorced for a number of years, she lives alone but takes care of her two grandchildren because both parents work. Diane has made friends with single women who enjoy movies, dining out, theater, and community activities. She is active in her church and a senior citizen group. She has done some international travel—South Korea, British Isles, Italy, France, Belgium, the Netherlands, and Germany. This travel has been enhanced because Diane has another daughter who teaches for the government overseas. Diane's health has been good, but she recently had a scare with her heart that resulted in a stint being placed in an artery. As a result, Diane has begun an exercise program.

One retiree said that he spends his time vacationing, spending quality time with family, and accepting life-changing health matters. Another person said that he spends time exercising, traveling, and working in his garden. During the summer, he grows vegetables and cuts lawns to make extra income. A male retiree said that he has become more involved in church work. He joined a recreation center for senior citizens with his wife, and they have Bible study and computer classes, and play games. He helps his wife around the house—cooking, cleaning, and yard work. A recent health concern was that he was diagnosed with colon cancer, but he reported that it was in remission.

Natalie after retirement was able to keep her grandson for the first eight months of his life. She also spends considerable time with her spouse of sixty years. As a missionary, Natalie has traveled in the United States and foreign countries. She reported a good quality of life prior to a recent illness.

A retired nurse said that her health has not been good over the past eight years, and she has undergone open heart surgery. However, she said that she and her husband have done some traveling, which she enjoys.

When Joan retired as a teacher in 2003, she dreamed of going to Puerto Vallarta, Mexico, and relaxing on the beach. She broke off a relationship with a retired male friend and traveled to Mexico. Joan enjoyed the summer on the beach, but in September took a two-month substitute teaching position at a private school in Mexico. When she returned home in October, she resumed her relationship with her retired male friend. They really enjoyed each other and had a wonderful time traveling, playing golf, and pursuing other recreational activities. Everything was going well for Joan until a year later, when her friend died from a heart attack.

She was devastated and became very depressed. Also, Joan developed some back problems as a result of playing golf. Friends tried to help and listen, but they were teachers and in school while she was retired. To be closer to her friends, Joan began substitute teaching at her old school. Also, she has been seeing a counselor and has begun to take medication for depression.

Chapter 6
The Role of Spirituality
in Retirement

The final question on the retirement questionnaire related to spiritual considerations in the retiree's life, and the question was stated in such a way that a response was optional. Almost all of the respondents chose to answer the question, and it seemed that spirituality and religion were important parts of their lives. Many of the retirees were very involved in their churches and service activities. One woman was director of music at her church and was involved in a day-care service for the church and community. Another woman said that she wanted to participate in church activities but at the time was working again because her pension was not enough to support her and her family. Of course, the retiree who was a pastor said that he was going to continue his studies in biblical counseling.

He said that he holds himself responsible for his congregation, community, and family. Another person said that she has a strong belief and faith in God. She prays every morning and believes that prayer truly works.

Many of the retirees said that they had been active in their churches for many years. Diane said that she was active in her church and that it is an important part of her life. She is a lector at mass and active in a senior citizens group, which offers opportunities to meet new people and become involved in community activities. Diane recently had a heart problem and was thankful for a good doctor, but she also turned to God in prayer. Another person said that for as long as she can remember, she has been active in church. As a teenager she accepted Jesus as her savior. Her lifestyle has been one of support for her family and friends. She believes that she has the gift to help others and will continue to serve as long as possible.

One male respondent said that from an early age he attended church regularly. However, he said that since retirement the spiritual aspect of life seems to have more meaning. He is grateful and thankful for the abundant life that God has given him. As he grows older and experiences the loss of old friends, the promise of eternal life is very comforting and helps him keep a positive attitude, lessening the dread of growing old. Another man said that he definitely consulted God before he decided to retire. God is first in his life, and he seeks God for all direction. He is thankful to God for allowing him to work for many years and for healing him of cancer so that he can enjoy life with his wife and family. A woman said that she was Catholic and has attended mass regularly with her husband. She became a Eucharistic minister and really enjoys serving in this capacity. Also, she reported that she and her husband when possible help others in need.

George said that he and his wife joined the LDS church in 1987. He never thought that he would become a Mormon, but the church means so much to them now and is the center of their lives. He said that he never understood the purpose of life before, but he now knows that he and his wife can be together for eternity. Another person said that he is a Christian and tries to practice his beliefs. "I have no expectations of rewards in this life other than the inner satisfaction of helping others," he told me. One retiree said that she and her son have home devotions with his children.

John said that he believes in prayer and consulting God before making any decisions in life. He believes that he is commissioned to share his faith at home, in the work place, and abroad. He said that his faith dictates his lifestyle and expectations.

Joan is the person who lost her gentleman friend a year after retirement and became depressed. She said that she has always believed that God was in control of her life. It was God who placed the retired gentleman in her life and showed her that she could enjoy a healthy relationship with a man. She said that she thinks that God will do it again when she is ready.

One person reported that he was a born-again Christian and that he has been very active in his church. Trying to follow Jesus has made a big difference in his personal and professional lives. His activities in the church and his beliefs have not changed since retirement. Another person reported that since he retired two years ago, he has had time to read the Bible and feels that he has become closer to God. He has had a chance to reflect on life and has become more spiritual.

One retiree reported a spiritual experience at age 26 that has affected his whole life. He decided that caring for his family and staying married was the most important thing in his life. He thanks God for this eye-opening experience, and today he serves in his church when his health permits.

In reviewing the retirees' responses to the spirituality and religion question, there seem to be some common themes:

* True obedience to God is from the heart.

* God calls us forth in love, concern, and helpfulness.

* God's salvation is eternal life.

* Discipleship is a full-time job.

* Sometimes what we need to do is not clear. We need to pray and listen to God.

* Church involvement and service are important in one's life.

* Prayer really works.

* Spirituality and religion become even more important after retirement.

These themes were repeated many times as the individuals talked about their retirement and life experiences. I think that health issues, the future, and the hope of eternal life were behind many of their responses.

Chapter 7
Planning for Retirement—
Case Studies

Several years ago I did a descriptive study of some individuals who had made career changes and were heading towards retirement. As a university professor, I worked with a couple of doctoral students who were interested in the factors that motivated individuals to make changes in their careers and how they might start thinking about retirement. We did in-depth interviews with a variety of people who were very willing to talk about their career changes. Subjects in the study were assured that their names would be kept confidential. The following case studies are based on these interviews but have been altered in some places to illustrate retirement concerns.

As you read these studies, I suggest that you might think about how each person began thinking about retirement.

What were their retirement goals, volunteer interests, travel plans, financial resources, recreational activities, and spiritual considerations?

Michael Sullivan

Michael Sullivan was an Episcopal priest who tried several careers before entering the priesthood and who also has made substantial career direction changes during his time in the priesthood. Born in Memphis, Tennessee, some sixty years ago, Michael Sullivan was the youngest of three children. His earliest memories were of life during the Great Depression. He remembered wearing hand-me-down clothes, especially a hand-knit green outfit that caused him a great deal of embarrassment as a first-grader. During Michael's early years, his father was in the laundry/dry-cleaning business and money was scarce. The family experienced considerable stress because of their limited resources. Michael remembered vividly, for example, how upset his father became one day when the dry-cleaning process ruined the dress of one of his best customers.

When the depression ended, Michael's father left the dry-cleaning business and went to work in the purchasing department of the Fisher-Body company in Memphis. During

World War II, Fisher-Body, a division of General Motors, manufactured B-25 bombers. At the end of the war, Michael's father was faced with the tough decision of moving with the company to Detroit or leaving Fisher-Body. When the family decided they did not want to leave Memphis, Michael's father took his severance pay and invested it in a men's clothing store. After two years in this business, however, he died of cancer, and the family sold his interest in the business. Michael remembers that his father's medical expenses consumed almost all of the profit from the sale. Michael's brother, the oldest of the three siblings, was completing a degree in mechanical engineering at the time of his father's death. Michael assumed the role of head of the household and helped his sister to complete a degree in teacher education.

Michael's family was very active in the Episcopalian Church. When he graduated from high school in 1948, the rector of his church, who had served as an effective and supportive role model for the church's young people, encouraged Michael to consider the ministry as a profession. With the encouragement of his priest, Michael entered a small Presbyterian college in Memphis with the intention of obtaining a liberal arts degree and then going on to seminary. When during Michael's sophomore year the rector of his family church died, Michael began to have doubts about his vocational choice, and at this point he changed his major to psychology. Looking back, Michael believes he was running from God and the church during this period of his life.

When he graduated from college, Michael took a job with the Bell Telephone Company as a trainee in the traffic department. His career at Bell was interrupted by a two-year stint in the Army during the Korean War. On returning to Bell Telephone, Michael was transferred to the engineering department in Louisville, Kentucky, where he worked in small towns outside the city. His job involved making cost estimates for repairs and overseeing subcontractors. Since he was not trained as an engineer, he was expected to learn on the job what he needed to know. Michael was not happy with this job, and also, he believed that the Holy Spirit was calling him back to the church.

Finally, Michael quit the telephone company job and returned to Memphis. At least in retrospect, he compares his return to that of the Prodigal Son. Although he did not immediately enter the ministry, he began to ease back into the church. For a short time, he held a job selling insurance, but the assistant rector of his church convinced him he would never be truly happy until he gave in to his calling.

Michael was 28 years old when he entered the seminary at the University of the South. He described his reaction to this change in his life as one of relief—"the chase was over; I was exhausted." Michael articulated his reasons for the career change very clearly: he was looking for intrinsic satisfaction; he wanted to work with people and to make a difference in their lives; he had achieved enough material success to recognize it was not all that important to him; and he felt he had been "called" to the ministry.

At the end of his first year in the seminary, Michael married, and at the end of his second year, he and his wife had their first child. Completing seminary in three years, Michael was assigned to several small churches in western Tennessee. From there he went to a midsize church in Pulaski, Tennessee, and, finally, to a large suburban church near Nashville. The move to the latter church was partially a result of the bishop's desire to help Michael secure special education facilities for his oldest son, who had by this time been diagnosed as dyslexic. When the special education program in Nashville proved inadequate, the Episcopal Church agreed to move Michael to Beaumont, Texas, where he had located a special school for learning disabled children. Here Michael became the associate pastor in a church with 1,400 members. The situation was less than ideal, however, because the senior pastor and the congregation were at odds. The senior pastor was relatively new, having replaced an eighteen-year veteran priest, who had been extremely popular within the church. Although the new pastor was a superb scholar, his personality and style did not mesh well with the expectations of his flock, and Michael was constantly placed in the role of peacemaker. Eventually the congregation forced the pastor to resign, and although Michael stayed on for several months with his replacement, Michael's disappointment with the behavior of the congregation caused him to begin looking for another church.

Finally, Michael found himself in Richmond, Texas, as the senior rector of a somewhat smaller church. Richmond is a small suburban town southwest of Houston. Here Michael became headmaster of a church-operated school (preschool through third grade) as well as rector of the church. This transfer was a wonderful opportunity for Michael and his family. Richmond was a growing community, and the church was growing with it. For nine years, Michael threw himself totally into working for the church and the community.

After nine years, Michael felt the effects of burnout, and he experienced a true midlife crisis where he felt unable to function in his chosen role. Fortunately for him, his bishop recognized the signs of overwork and too much responsibility and moved him to a position as a hospital chaplain in Houston. The new position gave him the opportunity to calm down, spend more time with his family, assess his own capabilities, and examine his life's goals and perspectives. At the end of two years, Michael felt he was ready to return to the parish priesthood. He moved back to Beaumont as the associate pastor of another church there. He no longer tried "to be all things to all people." He acknowledged that he had limits as a human being. For the first time, he experienced what it was like to really share responsibility with another priest and develop a "team ministry."

After eight years in the Beaumont church, Michael was approached by several other churches with offers to lead their parishes. The offer he accepted was in a small rural Texas town. It was a small church with a rich history. The sanctuary was small, chapel size, in fact, but it was a beautiful one-hundred-year-old replica of an English cathedral. Michael approached this position very differently than he had approached earlier appointments. He said he had finally learned that "I could not be God and save everyone." He learned to let the laypeople take more responsibility for church activities and programs; he saw his role more as catalyst or enabler, rather than as the one who must do everything. He was no longer looking for career advancement; in fact, he was beginning to consider retirement.

When we interviewed Michael, he was in his sixties and was starting to plan for retirement. The small rural church where he served as rector was only about fifty miles from Houston. He and his wife had many friends in Houston because he had spent a good part of his ministerial career working in the Houston area.

One of his goals for retirement was to let his wife choose where they would live. His thinking was that she never had an opportunity to select the town and house that they would live in because he always responded to a calling from a church and they lived in a house provided by the church. However, he felt that they would probably settle in the Houston area.

Michael also had a goal of continuing to serve God and the church on a part-time basis. He felt that there were many part-time and substitute opportunities because after retirement he would continue to be an Episcopal priest and perform all of the duties of a priest. Also, he talked about resuming some work as a hospital chaplain. God and the church would continue to be a very important part of his life.

Another goal that Michael had for retirement was to do some writing. His ministerial duties did not leave him much time for study and writing except for his sermons. He felt that he had a gift for writing and wanted to take advantage of the extra time offered by retirement.

Michael was going to receive an adequate retirement salary, but it was not going to be a large salary. In fact, his ministerial salary was never large, and his wife complained about his tendency to commit family resources to people in need when his family needed the money. Therefore, he talked about doing some traveling but felt limited by the availability of money.

One thing that Michael had not done was develop some hobbies other than reading, and he very rarely engaged in physical activities. He recognized that this was an area that needed some attention during retirement.

Michael's time at the small rural church was very rewarding, and the people really loved him. This situation was a good one for him to end his career as a minister. He felt very fulfilled and was looking forward to retirement.

Dorothy Montgomery

Dorothy Montgomery was in her forties when she decided to begin a career as a stockbroker. Dorothy was born and raised in southern Illinois. She described her family as a traditional family. Her father, who died in 1965, was a college graduate and a partner in an electrical company in Carbondale, Illinois. Her mother was a housewife. Her grandmother and great-grandmother, who she described as very independent women, supported themselves for many years by operating a hotel.

Dorothy has one brother, who is seven years younger than she. He is an attorney in South Carolina. Although not close as children due to the gap in their ages, Dorothy and her brother have become good friends as adults.

Music has always been an important part of Dorothy's life. She began piano lessons when she was four years old and cannot remember a time when she could not play the piano. She began giving piano lessons when she was fourteen years old. Later, to help support her education, Dorothy also worked as a piano accompanist and as a secretary. She attended college at Southern Illinois University in Carbondale, where she majored in applied music, graduating with honors in three years.

Shortly after completing her degree, Dorothy married Ronald, who was at the time working for the U.S. Forest Service in southern Illinois. Ron, who was three years older than Dorothy, had a forestry degree from Purdue University. Both Dorothy and Ron had ambitions to return to school for advanced degrees, but they decided that Ron should be the first to return. He chose the University of Wisconsin for masters and doctoral work in plant pathology. When Dorothy and Ron arrived in Madison, Dorothy began work as a typist on the University of Wisconsin campus. Later, her husband convinced her to take the Civil Service exam and get a better job with the U.S. Forest Service Laboratory. She began as a secretary but moved up to the position of laboratory assistant, a position she enjoyed very much.

As soon as Ron received his Ph.D., he was drafted into the Army. Dorothy joined him in West Palm Beach and began looking for a job. Because the job market was so tight there, she ended up accepting a Civil Service job at two grades below the position she had left in Wisconsin. They lived in Florida for nearly two years, and their first child was born during this time.

When Ron's military service was completed, they returned to Madison, where he accepted a job with the U.S. Forest Service Laboratory, and Dorothy began work on her master's degree in music at the University of Wisconsin. To augment the family income, she also taught private piano lessons. Her studies were briefly interrupted by the birth of her second child, but she completed her master's degree in two and a half years and accepted a part-time teaching position at the university.

After several years, Dorothy's husband was transferred to Minneapolis, where she continued to teach piano. A few years later, when the Forest Service wished to transfer him to Washington, D.C., Ron decided to consider other job possibilities. He ended up accepting a faculty position at a major university in central Texas.

When they moved to the small Texas community, Dorothy felt she had "moved to the ends of the earth." The community had little to offer in terms of cultural amenities, and the public school system seemed inferior to the Minneapolis schools where she was accustomed to sending her children.

Dorothy decided the only solution was to get involved and bring about some changes. She and another newcomer to the community, who also had extensive music training, decided to work together to get a music program in the schools. With the help of a local service organization, they began a concert series in the schools. They also formed an Arts Council, assisted in the formation of a community chorus, and brought together some instrumentalists for a presentation of Handel's *Messiah*, which eventually led to the formation of a community orchestra.

As a result of her community involvement, Dorothy was asked to become involved in writing a grant to the U.S. Department of Education seeking funds to provide cultural activities for underprivileged children in the community. When the grant was funded, she became the paid Executive

Director of the Arts Council Enrichment Program. In this role, Dorothy was successful in starting up an orchestra program in the schools—a program that is still successful today, long after the federal funds expired.

Although Dorothy could feel pride in some of her accomplishments for the Arts Council, her job, which depended on continued federal funding, did not offer very much security; nor did it pay particularly well. At about this time, Dorothy's husband quit his job at the university to begin a professional tree service business. Their two children were both in college, and Dorothy realized the family's economic security was at stake. She investigated some grant writing positions on the university campus. Then, a business that was in the same building as the Arts Council offered her a job selling retirement plans to university personnel. Before agreeing to accept their offer, however, she decided to talk to the only brokerage firm in town. Dorothy had always had an interest in investments; she had even taken a couple of investment courses when she lived in Minneapolis. Also, in Minneapolis, her personal investment counselor had told her that she had a real "knack" for the investment business.

When Dorothy contacted the brokerage office, they had never considered a woman broker. Her meeting with the manager was cordial, but he told her he was not hiring. The next day, however, he called her back and offered her a job. Dorothy accepted because she felt this position offered an opportunity for advancement and financial success.

Dorothy began working for the company in 1978. She began immediately to train for the New York Stock Exchange Test. The first part of her training involved a series of correspondence courses; this was followed by an intensive course at the brokerage home office in St. Louis. Because all of the material was new and different and also because it had been so many years since she had been involved in studying, Dorothy found the training very challenging. She said the test itself was the hardest she had ever taken, but she passed on the first try (which only 50% succeed in doing) and became a fully licensed stockbroker.

Dorothy said that the decision to become a stockbroker required considerable risk. She said, "I certainly did not want to be a middle-aged failure after having so many successes. I also did not want to be a visible failure. If you are a minority or a woman, you are more visible and have to be careful." She had no role model among her family or friends and little support. Dorothy said, "If I had said that I was going to be a prostitute, I don't think my mother would have been as shocked."

Dorothy said the first three years of her new career were very difficult. She was terrified of making mistakes and losing other people's money. Her office manager did not give her much help or support, and she found building a clientele to be a formidable task. She said she was ready to quit at the end of the first year, but she compensated for her insecurity and lack of support by working extra hard and working long hours.

Breaking into an all-male office was not without its problems either. For a while the broker in the next office made remarks like "all women should stay at home" and "girls should take home-economics courses." This broker was eventually fired for incompetence, however, and Dorothy said that overall she was lucky to have experienced very little discrimination or harassment based on her gender in spite of the fact that she was in a highly competitive business.

After the first three years, Dorothy began to reap the rewards of her hard work. She had a large and loyal clientele, and she was very successful. Her own financial net worth increased dramatically. Not only did she have financial resources, Dorothy also had a feeling of confidence and a feeling of self-sufficiency that she did not have previously. She also believes that she opened the door for other women stockbrokers in the community.

There were many aspects of her profession that Dorothy really enjoyed. She is a very achievement oriented and highly motivated person, and she enjoyed the fact that her success was measured in very tangible terms—number and profitability of investments. She also enjoyed the problem-solving aspects of the job and the opportunity to work with, and to help, people. She had a real sense of obligation when working with other people's money. Most of the time she was successful in helping her clients earn money, but obviously there were times when they had little profit or even lost money. She found, however, that most clients understood once they recognized that she was doing her best for them.

To be successful, Dorothy recognized that she had to make sacrifices. She worked long hours, and time commitments at home were often difficult. Had her children been younger, she could not have made the time commitment. She had to give up some of her community activities also, although she still found time for music and some volunteer work.

There were also some disappointments. Although she was not personally willing to give up any of the time she devoted to her clients to manage the office, she often wished that the office environment could be improved. When she was asked how her family felt about her career success, she said that she was not sure they knew that she was a success. Her mother could not identify with Dorothy's career: "She thinks I work too hard, and she really doesn't understand what I do." Her daughter, on the other hand, who, like Dorothy, has two degrees in music, is also a stockbroker. As for her husband, Dorothy feels that he was supportive of her career only up to the point where she started making considerably more money than he did. They have been divorced for a number of years.

Dorothy was the most successful broker in her office. She had numerous offers to move to larger cities and other firms, but she did not wish to leave her clientele. Dorothy felt that she was in control of her own destiny, and she liked her job so much that she did not want to retire even though she was at retirement age and had the financial resources to do so.

Dorothy Montgomery has been working for the same brokerage company for over 30 years and is in her seventies. She still is very successful at her work and is enjoying her work so much that she does not want to talk about retirement. A year ago, Dorothy had some serious health problems and missed work, but she has recovered and is back working long hours. She likes challenging and rewarding situations, and being a stockbroker offers those opportunities.

Her children have been grown and on their own for a long time. Dorothy lives by herself in a community that has long been home. She has many friends and attends concerts and other community activities. Dorothy is still a member of the Arts Council and several other community organizations. With significant financial resources, Dorothy takes several trips a year, including visits to her children. She also continues to be active in her church, and religion is an important aspect of her life.

Dorothy Montgomery does many of the things that a retired person would do—volunteer work, travel, church work, recreational activities, and spending time with her children, but she is not retired. Dorothy is a perfect example of Winston Churchill's advice: "Never, never, never retire."

Ellen Jones

Ellen Jones was a fifty-five-year-old Black woman who, for the first eighteen years of her adult life, worked as a manual laborer in a variety of jobs. Then, at the age of thirty-five, she decided to go to college and become a social worker. It was not easy; even after she obtained the degree, it took a long time to land a good permanent job, but she got that job and it brought a great deal of personal satisfaction.

Ellen was born in Longview, Texas; she was the fifth of nine children born to a mother and father she described as "just common laborers." Although Ellen's parents were not college educated, her maternal grandparents were. She recalls that her grandmother and grandfather were graduates of Wiley College and Paul Quinn College, respectively. At one point, her grandmother's brother was president of Paul Quinn. Although her own parents did not have college educations, they pushed their children toward formal education, as did her grandparents.

Ellen recalls that her dad's family was "self-made people," who made a better living than her mother's people. They had "pretty little white houses, picket fences, station wagons, and dogs—all the so-called comforts of life. Very few had children."

Ellen's father worked for a steel company, and her mother, who at eighty-five still resided in Longview, was a maid. Ellen said that although money was scarce, she did not realize they were poor until she grew up and others informed her of the fact—"we had a car; we all had a bed; and Mama sewed. There were also shared and separate responsibilities for each member of the family." Her home life was not happy, however, and she described her childhood as "a nice dysfunctional upbringing." When she was fourteen, her parents separated.

All of her siblings had some college experience. Two of her brothers were deceased; one sister operated a funeral home in Longview; one brother and one sister worked for General Dynamics in Fort Worth; one sister was in real estate, and another brother was in law school.

Ellen herself entered college at Texas Women's University right after high school, but when she became pregnant, her mother made her return home. She was married twice and had four children; all four had some college experience. Two had college degrees, one in psychology and one in business.

After years at various menial jobs, Ellen found herself working in a Jewish institutional home where she began as a nurse's aide. Although she was promoted to ward clerk after several months, she realized that was as far as she could go without a college degree. She could never be a nurse or a department head; nor could she ever significantly improve her salary. She recalls, "Something kept hammering at me. I was getting nowhere fast, and I was getting older, and I knew that I didn't want to be an old woman smoking cigarettes and doing physical labor."

Recognizing that a college education was the way out of her dead-end situation, Ellen decided to enroll at Texas Southern University in Houston. The decision was not an easy one, however. She deliberated for a long time and talked it over with all of her family members. Reactions were mixed. Her father and her children were elated and very supportive. Her mother, however, was negative about the idea—"you don't need to go to school; you need to stay on the job and help that man do something for the house." And her husband "didn't really care one way or the other just as long as I didn't waste the money."

Ellen relished the fact that most of her family supported her decision with enthusiasm. She also felt God played an important role in her choice: "He would not let me say I ain't gonna go. He kept pounding in my head that, Ellen, you have got to do something for yourself. Where are you going to be if something happens to your marriage—divorce, death, etc.? He just kept saying this is the choice I have made for you."

Entering TSU as an older student was to prove a real test for Ellen. When she received two F's the first semester, again she turned to God: "God didn't let me say, well, I'll just give up. He said, well, you'll do better next semester." Drawing on all of her strength and determination, Ellen persevered, and by the end of the first year, things began to improve. Eventually, she was so successful that she made the dean's list.

She discovered that being an older-than-normal student had some unexpected rewards as well. She could relate to much of her course work in ways that the younger, less experienced students could not. She recalls that when she talked about literature assignments in class, the instructor and her fellow students would just stop and listen. "I would tell them that it's just life. Sometimes I had to remind myself that I could be these children's grandmother, but that's life, too."

In spite of the age difference, Ellen was welcomed into the campus social life. She remembers playing cards and "hanging out" with band members, shakers (cheerleaders), athletes, and sorority and fraternity members. She was even invited to join several sororities. She jokes, "If my weight had been down, I would have tried out to be a shaker." To a surprising degree, Ellen was able to make up for what she had missed by dropping out of college. Two of Ellen's children were in college at the same time, and one was on the TSU campus with Ellen. Far from being a source of conflict, she found the shared experience enhanced her relationships with her children.

Ellen's husband, however, grew impatient with the time (five years) that it took for Ellen to complete her degree. Over time, he became less and less supportive and more frustrated with the demands on Ellen's time and attention. Although he supplied her with material support, he never offered encouragement or acknowledged any pride in Ellen's accomplishments.

Throughout the college experience, Ellen held on tight to a dream she had had for herself since high school—to become a social worker. Upon graduation, however, she found that a good social work job was not easy to find. She worked in the Houston public school system, in the emergency room at Ben Taub Hospital, and at the Mental Health and Mental Retardation Association. In the latter position, she did crisis counseling with the mentally ill. Later, she worked at Star of Hope (a home for the homeless). Although she really enjoyed the rewards of helping these people and gave each job "all she had," none of these jobs were permanent and none of them paid the professional wages she had anticipated.

Persevering in her characteristic way, in 1991, Ellen finally obtained a permanent position with the Social Welfare Department in Houston. Her job was to help accident victims as well as elderly and handicapped clients to become more self-sufficient. Ellen worked with clients directly, and she also had responsibility for arranging for other professional services that she identified as needed. Her clients included people of all ages who had car accidents, swimming mishaps, and gunshot wounds, people who had strokes or who were paraplegics. This was a dream come true for Ellen—she was able to help people find ways to improve their lives.

Finishing college and obtaining worthwhile employment changed Ellen's life dramatically. Shortly after she graduated from college, she and her husband divorced, an experience she described as getting rid of "baggage" that was weighing her down. She said that succeeding at her lifelong goals gave her "self-esteem plus." She did not allow anyone around her to feel bad because there are so many avenues to happiness and success. Ellen truly felt that she was more physically fit, emotionally mature, and more objective in her perceptions and actions than ever before in her life.

The only difficult adjustment resulting from her new independence was financial. She said, "The responsibility for paying all the bills and taking care of myself can sometimes be overwhelming, but with God's help, I manage."

Ellen's only regret was that her decision to return to college did not come earlier in her life. Her advice to anyone else considering a change was "Go for it; if you have one degree, go for another. If need be, get them all. Pitfalls will occur if you allow yourself to be sidetracked. Some pitfalls, however, can be constructive." And, finally, she added, "Get a big hand of God, and for whatever you want—the sky is the limit."

When we interviewed Ellen, she was just a few years removed from retirement age and would soon be thinking about retirement. She was thinking that she would retire when she reached the age of 65. Her income would include Social Security benefits and a pension from the Social Welfare Department. Since she now lived in her own home, she felt that she could live comfortably with this income. Ellen planned to spend as much time as possible with her children and grandchildren. She thought she might do some travel, but it was not a big priority. Volunteer work and church activities would be a big part of her life in retirement. Also, Ellen was a very socially oriented individual and looked forward to devoting more time to community organizations and causes.

John Holtz

This is the case of a successful bank trust officer who entered banking after eighteen years of experience in education. Born in 1928, John Holtz was raised in a small central Texas town. His father's occupation he described as "the cattle business, the grocery business, the lumber business, and eighteen years as the county sheriff." His mother, like other members of her family, was a schoolteacher, who was so dedicated to her profession that she was still substitute teaching at the age of seventy-five. John had one younger sister and an adopted brother. His sister was still a teacher in the town where John grew up, and her husband was the superintendent there.

John said that he always knew teaching was to be his vocation. It was a given; most of the people who influenced his life were teachers. He said, "All of my heroes were teachers. I wanted to talk like them; I wanted to be like them." Some members of his family, including his father, however, thought he should consider other career possibilities, particularly medicine or pharmacy.

Graduating from high school at sixteen, John attended a university in central Texas, where he majored in history and minored in chemistry with the objective of becoming a teacher. He was in the ROTC during college and was commissioned into the Army upon graduation. Unable to find a teaching job upon graduation and expecting to be drafted at any time, John, newly married to his high school sweetheart, Jean, decided to begin work on a master's degree in education. He also accepted a job at the Texas Company, later Texaco, to support himself and his new bride. He was, in fact, drafted after a year and served in Korea. After Korea, John stayed in the Reserves for thirty-three years, finally retiring as a full colonel.

When John returned home from Korea, he took a job as an assistant principal in a small east Texas town. In addition to his principal duties, John taught five subjects and was the girls' basketball coach and the substitute bus driver: "I was in heaven—it was just what I wanted to do."

Several years later, John, by now the father of two, moved to a school district closer to home, where he was first a junior high math and science teacher and coach, then a high school principal. He loved being involved in education at every level; he loved the kids, and he loved the teachers. His career trajectory in the school district was testimony to his effectiveness in education. Also during this time, John was preparing himself to become a public school superintendent by working on a doctoral degree in educational administration.

At the end of the school year, after fifteen successful years in the school district, one day the well-respected president of a fairly young, up-and-coming local bank asked John to lunch and offered him a job in the trust department of the bank. Although he was flattered at being singled out by someone known for his business acumen and personal integrity, John's initial reaction was "thanks a lot, but I'm really not interested."

When he went home that evening and told his family about the unusual event in his day, they reacted by strongly urging him to at least consider the offer. John said the sixties were hard on school administrators, and he believes that his family was perhaps more aware than he himself of the stresses he was experiencing. A high school principal could never really leave the school and the sense of responsibility for it behind, and in the era of greater than normal campus and student unrest, the burden was heavy. John believes that his family was also probably more influenced than he by the prospect of the prestige and lifestyle offered by a career in banking. Interestingly enough, John's father, who had urged him to consider other possibilities as a young man, wondered at John's judgment in abandoning a successful career to pursue one in a field about which he knew nothing.

After two days of consideration, John did decide to make the career change. He was excited by the challenge. At the time, banking had a very good image, and he was pleased with the prospect of providing a more affluent lifestyle for his family. The most important single factor in his decision, however, was the solidity of the man who hired him: "I probably would not have made the change for someone else." But John knew two things for sure: "The bank under this president's leadership would be a successful enterprise, and the man's judgment was sound enough that if he believed I could do the job, I could."

The transition period was not easy, however. At forty years old, John was a knowledgeable, successful public school educator, with only a few rungs of the professional ladder left to climb. He had the experience and the credentials; in fact, he received his Ph.D. in education a few months after entering the bank. And then suddenly, he found himself at the very bottom in a field in which he was totally ignorant. His first assignment was to attend a three-week graduate school of banking at SMU. All of his fellow students were graduates of business schools, lawyers. and bankers. John said, "They still talk about me at that school!" It was not the typical way to embark on a banking career.

John discovered that he had not only accepted the challenge of learning a new field, but also the challenge of building a trust department almost from scratch. When he entered the bank, the trust department had assets of just fewer than one million dollars. Today, twenty years later, it has 112 million in assets and is expanding rapidly. John was on the bank's board of directors and was, self-admittedly, one of the five most influential officers in the bank.

John said that in spite of his initial ignorance of banking, he was never really afraid of failing. The personal philosophy that worked for him in education served him well in banking also: "If you work hard and make good decisions, things will work out."

John found satisfaction in his career as a banker. His family was always happy with the career change, with the enhanced prestige and with more economic security. John was quick to point out, however, that the difference between his salary and that of a superintendent of a large school district was not actually very great because of the hard times banking had gone through in recent years. However, he admitted that there were other perks, like a company car, country club membership, and superior employee benefits.

The greatest satisfaction of his banking career came from his sense of accomplishment. He succeeded in mastering a new field. He even returned as an instructor to the banking graduate school where he had his first "baptism by fire" into the banking world. And he succeeded at building a strong trust department. Not only did the department increase in size under his tenure, but its image and reputation were enhanced substantially. He was especially proud of the number of people who come to him to set up trusts to manage their money after death; as he said, "What greater trust could there be than that?"

Although he changed professions twenty years earlier, John never completely gave up his love for, and involvement with, education. He served as an elected member of the local school board for many years, and then he was a member of the board of directors of the local Education Service Center, a regional office of the Texas Education Agency.

John was at retirement age when we interviewed him, and his position at the bank would provide him with good retirement benefits. He was also thinking about ways to remain active after retirement. One activity was to remain as a director of the Education Service Center.

The church was very close to John and his wife. He served on the board of trustees and the finance committee and frequently taught an adult Sunday school class. These were activities that John planned to continue. John and his wife were also active in community volunteer activities. They had two children and several grandchildren, and they wanted to spend more time with their family.

Because John's work kept them so busy, they did not have much time for travel. There were many places in the United States and other countries that they wanted to visit. John liked to hunt and fish and play golf. These were activities that John wanted to spend more time pursuing during retirement

Chapter 8
Making Retirement a
Positive Adventure

‖‖

Part of making retirement a positive experience is developing a plan. Depending on your job circumstances and your financial situation, planning may or may not be possible. Even if you have already retired, it is not too late to have a plan. It is usually a good idea to let people know that you are going to retire unless it might jeopardize your job situation. Sometimes the offer of a good retirement package or some other development at work may cause an unplanned retirement. The bottom line is to develop a retirement plan.

Of course, planning can enhance the possibility that you will have an adequate income when you retire. My wife and I had been paying into retirement funds for years, and we were eligible for Social Security benefits. We also had the services of a financial planner who was very competent and trustworthy. It is very important that a financial planner puts your interest ahead of his interests. Since retirement, our income has been more than adequate, and I can say that we and our financial planner did a good job.

Having a good health care program is an important part of a retirement plan. As you get older, usually you will require more medical care. So far, we have not had any major illnesses, but we have had medical bills that have been covered by our medical insurance. Without proper insurance, a major illness has the potential of wiping out your savings.

A major decision for retirement is where you are going to live. Are you going to continue to live in your present home, or move somewhere else? Before moving, be very careful in exploring the location, living conditions, and costs, and deciding if you will miss friends and family. This is a decision that requires time and considerable thought. Factors will vary for individuals depending on their health, finances, and family conditions.

When you retire, you may have difficulty in leaving your job and friends. One way of transitioning to retirement is to continue in your field of work. When I retired, I continued to teach part-time at a local university. For many individuals, staying active in their fields, at least at a reduced rate, is a good idea. It is said that the sudden silence gained by retiring from a demanding job into a life of idleness is not healthy. Not having a schedule or deadlines to meet can be a good feeling, but boredom is a major cause of dissatisfaction with retirement.

Retirement can offer an opportunity to launch a new career. There may be some type of job or activity that you have wanted to do for many years but did not have the time or resources to accomplish. Now may be the time to start that new career. Work is important, whether it is paid or unpaid. There are many volunteer opportunities that can be very rewarding.

Some retirees go back to school and take courses that they did not have time for previously. I have known individuals who decided to go back to school to complete a degree program that they started many years earlier. This can be a rewarding and invigorating experience. Some people develop talents that they did not know that they had. The following statement may give you something to think about: "People don't care what you did, but they care about what you are doing now."

In my survey of retirees, I found that spiritual development and church participation were important components of their lives. There are many aspects of religion that can make life more meaningful and enjoyable:

1. Increased capacity to love self and others
2. The ability to reach out and help others
3. The belief of many that discipleship is a full-time job to be placed above all others
4. Strong belief in God and the power of prayer
5. Belief that God's salvation is eternal life
6. Bible study
7. Satisfaction gained through helping others

Longevity is related to a person's attitude and lifestyle, and the quality of a person's retirement has to do with how they approach life. A preacher friend of mine said that there is a belief that older people naturally get more cranky and difficult to get along with. However, he said that he has found that angry elderly people were that way long before they became old. We cannot be perfect and always pleasant, but there are many personal qualities that add to a happy life:

1. Basic optimism
2. Adaptability
3. Healthy self-esteem
4. Forgiveness
5. Sense of humor
6. Positive attitude about aging

We cannot always control our health and the illnesses that we may encounter, but there are many things that we can do to live a healthier life. Experts say that 25 percent of a person's longevity is controlled by heredity and 75 percent by lifestyle. Eating healthy food and controlling your weight can improve your health. Before I retired, I jogged and exercised, but I was overweight and out of shape. I have been retired a little over four years, and I began an exercise program right after I retired. Since retirement, I have lost forty pounds and exercise almost every day. For three to four days a week, I spend two hours per day at a gym working on weight machines and riding a recumbent bicycle. The other days, I ride my bicycle around the community for approximately fifty minutes. Physically, I feel much better and like the exercise activities. Also, I have developed several friendships with people whom I have met at the gym. I am not a smoker and very rarely have an alcoholic beverage, so these are not problems for me, but both smoking and drinking can obviously contribute to poor health. Addictive behaviors in older adults can be a real problem, and many times friends and family tend to overlook these behaviors. If you have an addictive behavior, you need to address the issue and seek help if you need it.

A recent article in the *Houston Chronicle* reported on a study of older people by researchers at Chicago's Rush University Medical Center. This study reported that elderly people who see themselves as self-disciplined, organized achievers have a lower risk for developing Alzheimer's disease than people who are less conscientious (Johnson 2007). A purposeful personality protects the brain against mental decline; many researchers suggest that older people should stay active both physically and mentally.

There are many factors that contribute to and influence the activities of retirees. One of the first factors is income and living conditions. If you have an adequate income, travel is a good possibility, especially if there are places that you always wanted to visit. We have taken two ocean cruises and are booked for a river cruise through central Europe this summer. Taking a cruise was something that we had never done. Also, we have done some traveling in the United States, including Alaska and Hawaii. It is wise to travel while your health and mobility permit.

If you are fortunate enough to have grandchildren, it is time to enjoy them. Two of our granddaughters live very close to us. Another granddaughter lives an hour away. Our first grandson is sixteen months old and lives in California with his parents. We visit them two to three times a year, and they also visit us. I think that being with them keeps us young, and we really have fun together.

Keeping in touch with old friends can be a rewarding experience, and you can share ideas about retirement activities and feelings. A former university colleague lives about thirty minutes from my house, so we have lunch together occasionally. My wife, a former teacher, keeps in close contact with friends at her former school almost every day by e-mail. Although the school is in another town about three hours away, they get together several times a year.

The ultimate objectives in your retirement should be a good quality of life and enjoyment. Retirement is a new experience and should offer many enjoyable opportunities— new career experiences, travel, golf, grandchildren, new learning opportunities, volunteer work, helping others, exercise, entertainment, and reading, to mention a few.

Part of making retirement an exciting adventure is to develop a plan. A first step might be to assess how you spend your time each day. The following chart can help if you write down your activities hour by hour for an entire week. This chart (Figure 1) will show how you prioritize activities and interests. Completing the Planning Questionnaire (Figure 2) that follows can assist in developing a retirement plan.

The best way to make your retirement an adventure that is meaningful and rewarding is to have a plan. I hope that my ideas and experiences will help you make retirement an adventure.

Figure 1

Record of Daily Activities

	Sunday	Monday	Tuesday	Wed.	Thursday	Friday	Saturday
1:00 AM							
2:00 AM							
3:00 AM							
4:00 AM							
5:00 AM							
6:00 AM							
7:00 AM							
8:00 AM							
9:00 AM							
10:00 AM							
11:00 AM							
Noon							
1:00 PM							
2:00 PM							
3:00 PM							
4:00 PM							
5:00 PM							
6:00 PM							
7:00 PM							
8:00 PM							
9:00 PM							
10:00 PM							
11:00 PM							
Midnight							

Figure 2

Planning Questionnaire

1. Retirement Goals (e.g., staying active, healthy, keeping mind alert, participating in worthwhile activities, having fun, etc.)

2. Volunteer Interests

3. Travel Destinations

4. Learning Activities

5. Financial Resources and Concerns

6. Recreational Activities

7. Physical Activities

8. Spiritual Considerations and Activities

9. Nurturing Relationships (family and friends)

10. Cultural Activities (exploration and continuation)

11. Specific Interest Areas to Research and Study (possibly a personal library)

12. Hobbies or Collections to Develop or Continue

Addendum

I mentioned earlier in the book that I was thinking about discontinuing my part-time teaching. The university was undergoing some changes; the dean who had hired me had retired, and the acting department head whom I had known for many years had gone back to full-time teaching. The new department head wanted me to teach a third course and teach on Saturday mornings. These were two things that I did not want to do. After three and one-half years of teaching and enjoying the students, I decided that it was time to quit and look at some other endeavors.

Church and intensive Bible study have become important parts of my life. At one of the Bible study groups, I became friends with a couple who were very involved in volunteer activities related to the church and community. Barbara is a retired nurse who was taking training to become a hospital lay chaplain at a training program in the Houston Medical Center. She told me about the training experiences and talked me into applying to the program. I took the six-month training program and now work as a lay chaplain one day a week at a local hospital. I really enjoy the work and feel that I am helping people. Also, this chaplain program fits well with my counseling background.

I keep in touch with friends via e-mail and the telephone. Occasionally, I have lunch with a former colleague who lives in the Houston area. He has had some health problems, so sometimes we just talk on the phone. Also, two of our granddaughters live about fifteen minutes away, so we see them frequently. My wife picks them up from school and takes them to dance, swimming, and gymnastics.

The most significant change that has occurred since I started writing this book has been health related. About seven to eight months ago, I was having prostate problems and ended up having surgery. The operation went well, and I think that I am back to normal in terms of my prostate.

The other health issue relates to my knees and a lack of mobility. I mentioned earlier that my wife and I were planning a Danube river cruise. Well, the trip was wonderful, but after about two days, my knees were bothering me so much that I could barely walk. When we returned from the trip, I visited an orthopedic surgeon, and three weeks ago I had my first knee replacement surgery. The surgery went well, and I think that I am making excellent progress. The plan is to have the second knee replaced in four to six months.

I plan to resume my volunteer activities and get back to my routine at the gym as soon as possible. My wife and I plan to do more traveling as soon as my knee heels.

References

Bryan-College Station Eagle. 1985. Talk about a change of pace. June 4.

Christoffersen, John. 2007,. More older workers deciding it's not time to clock out just yet. *Houston Chronicle,* 15 August, A3.

Freedman, M. 2001. The new unretirement: The fine art of making a second career your life's work. *Modern Maturity,* January–February,53–63.

Johnson, C. K. 2007. Alzheimer's risk tied to personality traits/ conscientious achievers are less prone to disease, research suggests. *Houston Chronicle,* 2 October, A1–A2.

Mahoney, David and Restak, Richard. 1998. <u>The longevity strategy: How to live to 100 using the brain-body connection.</u> New York: John Wiley & Sons, Inc.

McShane, Larry. 2005. One man, one quest—1,000 bars in one year. *Houston Chronicle*, 29 May, A3.

Walker, Lou Ann. 2001. We can control how we age. *Parade Magazine*, 16 September, 4–5.

About the Author

||||||||||||||||||||||||||||||||||||||||||||||||||||||||||||||||||||||||||||||||||||||||||||||||||||||||||||||||||||||||||||||||||||||||

Chris Borman lives in Houston with his wife, Ruth. He stays active through volunteer work such as serving as a lay chaplain at a local hospital. Chris enjoys spending time with his three daughters and their families (three granddaughters and one grandson). He is Professor Emeritus at The University of Texas–San Antonio. Chris also was on the faculty in Counseling Psychology at Texas A&M University (College Station) for twenty-one years. His research and writing have been in the areas of career development and career counseling.